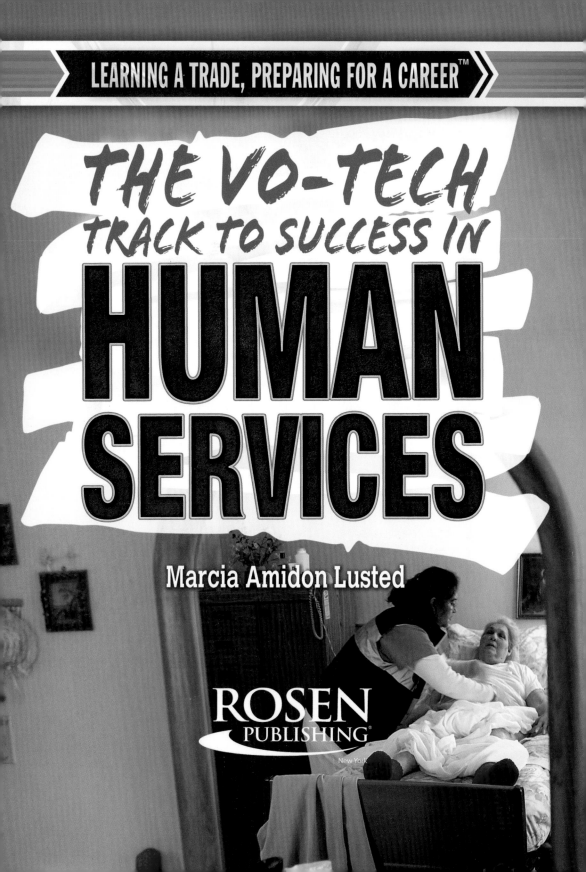

LEARNING A TRADE, PREPARING FOR A CAREER™

THE VO-TECH
TRACK TO SUCCESS IN
HUMAN SERVICES

Marcia Amidon Lusted

ROSEN
PUBLISHING®
New York

Published in 2015 by The Rosen Publishing Group, Inc.
29 East 21st Street, New York, NY 10010

Copyright © 2015 by The Rosen Publishing Group, Inc.

First Edition

Library of Congress Cataloging-in-Publication Data

Lusted, Marcia Amidon.
The vo-tech track to success in human services/Marcia Amidon Lusted.
       pages cm.—(Learning a trade, preparing for a career)
Includes bibliographical references and index.
ISBN 978-1-4777-7732-9 (library bound)
1. Human services—Vocational guidance—Juvenile literature. I. Title.
HV40.L97 2015
361.0071′5—dc23

                                        2013051158

Manufactured in the United States of America

CONTENTS

Introduction   4

Chapter One:
A Helping Hand   8

Chapter Two:
Is Human Services Right for Me?   18

Chapter Three:
A Day in the Life   29

Chapter Four:
Exploring Your Vo-Tech Options   42

Chapter Five:
Vo-Tech and Beyond   55

Glossary   66

For More Information   68

For Further Reading   70

Bibliography   72

Index   77

INTRODUCTION

By the time they reach high school, many teens are already working part-time. Some may have jobs in fast-food restaurants or retail stores. Others may babysit or mow lawns. But some students may already be doing jobs that they'd like to turn into careers. Some may work with the elderly, as an assistant to someone with a disability, or in a homeless shelter. They may do this work through a volunteer program. Perhaps they are paid to work in a nursing home or day care facility. Or they may simply be helping out an elderly neighbor having trouble doing everyday tasks.

Jobs like these may start out as just something to do to make a little money or earn community service credits for school. Often, however, these experiences give teens their first taste of what could become a permanent career in the field of human services. Some teens may discover that they really like working with the elderly. Some may learn they have an aptitude for working with young children or people with mental illnesses. Others may be intrigued by careers working with former prison inmates or helping new immigrants find jobs and adjust to their new lives.

How can teens take an interest in human services and turn it into a career? Today's students are lucky to have the vo-tech, or vocational-technical, option.

This student is working with the elderly on an art project. Volunteering may help teens develop an interest in a career in human services.

While they are still in high school, they can start learning about and preparing for a vocation. They can start those careers as soon as they graduate or even beforehand. Vocational education in high school has become an increasingly important means of educating students for the real world of jobs. It can help students step into that world better prepared and with more options than ever before—without necessarily having to earn a four-year college degree.

What do jobs such as working with children, the elderly, the disabled, or immigrants have in common? They are all part of a category of careers known as social and human services. Workers in this field help people when they are facing difficult times or unusual circumstances or if they need more support than they can get from their families. Human services jobs are usually found in nonprofit organizations, social service agencies, and state and local governments.

Workers with the skills for human services jobs are in demand. According to the Bureau of Labor Statistics, from 2012 to 2022, the number of jobs for social and human service assistants is expected to grow by 22 percent, much faster than the average for all careers. And while many careers in human services require two- or four-year college degrees or even more advanced degrees, many positions require only a high school diploma. Social and human service assistants, for example, can work hands-on with clients. However, they don't need postsecondary schooling or degrees to get started. In fact, for people interested in the human services field, chances are good that they can get started on a career before they even leave high school. A career as an assistant in the human services field does not necessarily require attending college and finding a way to pay for it. But it does mean taking advantage of a resource that might be available for free from a student's own high school or a school nearby.

What is this hidden resource? Some teens believe that by the time they are nearing the end of high school, there isn't much left for school to offer them in terms of courses that will have real-world usefulness. But that isn't the case. Since 2006, the Carl D. Perkins Career and Technical Education Act has required states to provide programs of study in career and technical education. This means that teens who want to transition right into jobs after high school—or start their career with less than four years of college—can have access to classes that will help them prepare for those jobs. No matter where teens attend high school in the United States, their school or one close by is likely to offer vocational education. And for those who want to start working in the human services field immediately upon graduation or soon after, a vo-tech program will give them the tools they need to get started right away.

Chapter One

A HELPING HAND

Just what is meant by "human services"? This term refers to a field that helps meet human needs. It helps people deal with challenges in their environment, including home, school, and work, in a more functional, productive way. One person may be disabled and have trouble dealing with everyday tasks at home. Another may have an addiction to drugs or alcohol and have difficulty holding down a job. Low-income parents who are finding it hard to feed their children may need help getting food stamps. These are all examples of people who might be helped by someone working in the human services field. Human services work focuses not only on dealing with existing problems, but also on trying to prevent issues in the future.

The field of human services covers many different types of jobs in a variety of settings. It might mean working for a local, state, or federal government agency. It might mean working for a nonprofit organization or inside a correctional institution, hospital, or rehabilitation facility. Since human services is a broad category, there are many different options for people who want to work in this field.

Jobs in Human Services

Human services is a broad career category. Some jobs require years of college education and even graduate school. Other jobs can be done with just a high school diploma, a technical certificate from a community college, or an associate's degree. Entry-level jobs, such as a job as a human services assistant, may be a good way to get started in the field and may lead to other positions.

What are some of the specific jobs that fall into this category? Generally speaking, the higher-level positions for a career in human services include counselors, psychologists, social workers, and sociologists.

Many vo-tech schools encourage prospective students to visit and see their programs firsthand before applying to attend.

Counselors give advice and help to people who are just starting out or who need some help getting back on their feet after a financial or emotional setback. There are specialties for counselors, such as guidance counselors who help students plan their futures or substance abuse counselors who help people overcome addictions.

Psychologists are professionals who study human behavior. They may work with patients or groups in a clinic or private practice. They may work in research laboratories, universities, or schools. They may even work in industry with employees or in marketing.

Social workers are some of the most hands-on human services workers. They generally work directly with clients, often in their homes and communities, although some work in research or management jobs. They typically work for government agencies, nonprofit organizations, health organizations, or schools.

Finally, sociologists focus more on research than on working with people. Sociologists study human behavior, political systems, and cultural change. Their research findings can help other human services workers, government agencies, and educators make better decisions.

In addition, for every position that requires advanced education, such as a social worker or substance abuse counselor, there is usually an aide or assistant to support that position.

Human services assistants can have many specific job titles. These include social work aide or assistant, family services assistant, substance abuse counselor aide, caseworker aide, and human services worker.

What Do Human Services Workers Do?

It can be easier to distinguish among human services jobs by looking at the different categories of people they serve.

Some human services workers focus on families and children. They make sure that children live in safe homes. They help families in need get public assistance such as welfare or food stamps. If fam-

Human services workers, such as this nurse, often assist young mothers and their babies in their homes.

ilies need housing or child care, human services workers can help them find those resources.

Other human service employees work with elderly people to keep them in their own homes as long as possible, providing assistance with housekeeping or personal care. When elderly clients can no longer remain in their homes, they may assist them in finding a residential facility where they can live.

Like the elderly, people with disabilities also require support from human services workers. These workers provide help adapting clients' homes to accommodate their disabilities. They may provide assistance with daily living needs, such as making meals or taking baths.

For people struggling with substance abuse, human services workers help clients find programs where they can overcome their addictions. They may guide them to an appropriate support group or one-on-one counseling. If the addiction is extreme or life threatening, they may help a client find a residential facility.

Human services workers also help military families and veterans. They may help those with an enlisted family member manage the separation from their loved one. They may assist

someone who has been discharged from the military in finding housing or a job. They also connect older veterans with the services they might need, such as medical care or transportation.

This human services worker counsels a young veteran at a mental health treatment center.

People struggling with mental health issues are also helped by human services workers. They work with clients to find support groups or one-on-one counseling. They may locate a group home or residential facility if a client cannot take care of himself or herself.

Immigrants who are new to the United States also benefit from human services help. Human services workers may help immigrants find a job or a place to live. They also support them in adjusting to a new country and a new way of life. They may connect clients with resources for learning to speak English or provide legal assistance with paperwork and citizenship issues.

People who have recently been released from correctional facilities, such as prisons, may need support finding jobs or entering job-training programs. Human

HOW MANY?

According to the Bureau of Labor Statistics, social and human services assistants held 384,210 jobs in 2010. About 21 percent were employed in individual and family services, 16 percent in nursing and residential care facilities, and 13 percent in community and vocational rehabilitation services. About 24 percent worked in state and local government agencies.

services workers can help them find a place to live and start fresh lives in society.

Finally, homeless people often benefit from interaction with human services workers. They may receive help with basic needs, such as finding refuge in a homeless shelter or getting a meal from a soup kitchen. They may also get help finding a job and a permanent place to live.

Because of the wide variety of jobs and settings, human services workers have many options for where, when, and how much they want to work. Some may work at office jobs with a set schedule in a regular location. Others may spend their days traveling from place to place within their community. Working full-time or part-time, meeting in clients' homes or in a social services agency, working regular daytime hours or overnight shifts, there are many possibilities. Due to the aging population of the United States, over time there will be more elderly, veterans, and disabled people, as well as the continuing problems of homelessness, mental illness, and family issues. Because of this, the human services field is only going to keep growing.

So What Do I Do First?

If a student likes the idea of working with people and helping them, then a career in human services may be the career path for him or her. The good news is that getting started in this field is something that even a high school student can do. It isn't necessary to wait until after graduation or spend several years getting

High school students in vo-tech programs can take classes in human services subjects before they even graduate.

an associate's or bachelor's degree before beginning to work.

School districts are required to provide vocational and technical training programs for students who are interested in moving right into a job after graduation. This means high school students can take classes that will pave the way for an entry-level human services job. Working at this level can be a student's permanent career choice. It can also be a way to get started on a career path leading to higher education and a job at a more advanced level.

In order to get the most out of a vocational training program and be prepared for a job after high school, students need to identify what aspect of human services interests them most. After exploring the broad categories, it helps to look at some of the specific jobs and what they involve. Some jobs can be done with minimal specialized education. Others require training beyond high school or a college degree and might be something to aspire to for someone who enters the field with an entry-level job.

Chapter Two

IS HUMAN SERVICES RIGHT FOR ME?

One way to decide whether human services is a good fit is to look at the tasks and responsibilities of typical jobs in the field. Students need to think about whether they would enjoy these tasks and do them well. Students also need to identify what population they see themselves working with. Finally, students need to decide what kind of setting they would most enjoy working in. For example, a student may decide he or she would like to do social work with the elderly. Would he or she be happiest working in an institution, such as a nursing home or rehabilitation center, or in the community, visiting clients' homes?

The following are typical job tasks and working environments of some of the most common jobs in human services.

Social Worker or Caseworker

Social workers are some of the most visible and familiar workers in the human services field. They fulfill an important role in connecting people to solutions and resources. "People need your help and if you're part of the human race, you give it to them," one social worker commented on the Princeton Review's website, adding, "The only strange thing is that you get paid to do it."

There are several types of social workers. For students interested in the vo-tech path to human services, it is important to know the difference, since social workers often require assistants and aides. Direct-service social workers work with people to help them solve problems in their lives and cope with everyday situations and tasks. Clinical social workers diagnose mental, emotional, and behavioral problems. Caseworkers are a subcategory of direct-service social workers. They are usually responsible for a caseload of specific clients. They visit or meet with their clients

Social workers often work with members of the military and their families, helping them with education, finances, and child care issues.

and help find them the resources they need to function well and cope with problems.

A direct-service social worker usually starts by identifying people who need help. They may have certain unmet needs or disabilities. The social worker has to assess these and determine what is needed to help each person achieve his or her goals. Goals might include continuing to live independently or to get child care or health services. The social worker devises a specific plan to meet each goal. He or she may need to locate community resources for the client, such as food stamps or free health care. The social worker may help the client apply for these benefits, especially if he or she works for a state or government agency.

Direct-service social workers must be available in case a client suffers a personal crisis, natural disaster, or abusive situation. They need to continually follow up with their clients. They also need to evaluate the services or resources offered to the client and make sure that they are effective. Such social workers typically interact with many different types of people, unless they specialize in a certain population such as children or the elderly. They may have to help clients in distressing situations, such as cases of child abuse or terminal illness. They may also work with clients who are distrustful or aggressive.

Clinical social workers treat mental illnesses and disorders such as anxiety, depression, and behavioral problems. They also help people going through difficult times, such as a divorce or a death in the family. They diagnose clients' issues and create appropriate treatment programs for them, sometimes in consultation with doctors or other health care professionals. Clinical social workers may treat clients individually or in group therapy sessions. They must constantly monitor their clients' progress and adjust their treatment if necessary. In some cases, they may refer their clients to other resources or services. They also have to do administrative work such as recordkeeping and dealing with insurance.

Both direct-service and clinical social worker jobs require at least a bachelor's degree, and becoming a clinical social worker may also require a master's degree. Both of these career positions require assistants or aides, who can start out with just a high school diploma. These assistants help with recordkeeping, researching available client benefits and services, conducting support programs, and visiting clients in their homes. Someone interested in becoming a social worker can get a good feel for the job by working as a social work assistant.

Life Skills Instructor

Another type of human services job is that of a life skills instructor. These instructors teach people how to manage everyday tasks that they are struggling with. The clients may be children, teens, or adults. The instructor helps clients gain independence and move forward in life by mastering basic life skills such as hygiene, cooking, cleaning, self-protection, and dealing with money. They may work with people one on one or in groups.

A life skills instructor may work with young people who do not yet have these skills or with adults who never learned them. Judy Belmont, a life skills educator for adults, writes in her blog, *Belmont Wellness*, "Teaching life skills is not telling clients what to do— it is teaching them strategies that they have never learned in school or in life. This proactive approach empowers clients with tools for life, and helps them experience change constructively."

Life skills instructors are expected to have knowledge in the area they are teaching, and they may have to demonstrate this knowledge in order to get a job. In some cases, they may need certification, such as if they are working in a school setting. In other cases, such as helping people learn or relearn how to drive a car, all that may be required is a driver's license and a clean driving record. The level of education or certification required depends on the skills that the instructor will be teaching. It also depends on the clients. If a life skills instructor is going to work with disabled or special needs children, for example, he or she must have training and experience working with these kinds of students.

Life skills instructors can work in many different settings. They can work in schools, therapy agencies, treatment centers, group-housing settings, and prisons. They can also work for private companies or charities. Life skills instructors may work with specific populations, such as senior citizens who are trying to regain independence after medical problems or young people who are learning how to get jobs. They need to be good communicators and have patience, since some clients may become easily frustrated. Some clients may be angry about their situations and their need to adjust to new circumstances.

Community Organizer

A community organizer, also known as a community action worker, is another job within human services. This job involves working collectively with people, usually in a community or neighborhood, to solve problems. It might mean joining with or creating an organization to address an issue that concerns people in their com-

A community organizer assists immigrant workers with their computer skills.

munity or workplace. It might mean helping people with an interest they share, such as housing or economic development.

Community organizers are often involved in community development and social planning. They work to empower people to solve their own problems by coming together and cooperating on a solution. Community efforts might include planning a new health center, getting a drug dealer to move out of a city block, raising funds to build a senior center, finding volunteers to work in a women's shelter, or raising public awareness about homelessness.

Many community organizers start out because they are committed to a specific cause or are even concerned about something taking place in their own neighborhood. Some get started with volunteer work. Anthonine Pierre, lead community organizer at the Brooklyn Movement Center, told the *Idealist Careers* blog, "I believe in volunteering on principle, but strongly recommend it for people interested in community organizing. You have to learn to navigate the various organizations working on policy and on-the-ground change, and you have to learn how to connect with the people you serve."

Others get started by joining federal government programs such as AmeriCorps VISTA or the Peace Corps. Community organizers do not necessarily have to have a college degree. However, organizations that hire community organizers welcome people with degrees in social sciences or human services. They might even give financial support to a worker who is interested in pursuing a degree.

BEFORE HE WAS FAMOUS

One of the most famous people to have worked as a community organizer is President Barack Obama. From 1985 to 1988, he worked as director of the Developing Communities Project in Chicago. One of his tasks was interviewing workers who had lost their jobs in order to evaluate their skills and help them find new positions. He helped set up a summer jobs program for teenagers in their neighborhood on the South Side of Chicago. He also worked with the Chicago Housing Authority to remove asbestos from an older housing project in the area. In addition, he helped set up a college prep tutoring program, a job training program, and a tenants' rights organization.

Before he served as U.S. president, Barack Obama worked as a community organizer in Chicago. This experience was a valuable foundation for his political career.

Group Activities Aide

In a nursing home, residential facility, or group home, aides are often hired to support an activities leader or director. The director is responsible for creating and running group recreational activities. These might be fun, leisure activities, but often they also have a purpose, such as improving dexterity, encouraging movement, stimulating mental activity, or promoting social interaction. Activities can include exercise routines, arts and crafts, music, drama, and even sports. They can also include field trips and outside activities. Activities directors and aides often plan holiday activities, as well as produce a newsletter for patients, staff, and families.

Working as a group activities aide is an important role, especially in a nursing home, where well-planned activities can be a lifeline for residents. Kay Paggi writes on Caring.com, "Imagine yourself in a nursing home. Here the activities available to you may include Bingo, an afternoon tea party, trivia, or a beanbag toss. Wow. Is it any wonder that most residents in nursing homes are depressed and have cognitive

An activities aide in a nursing home helps an elderly resident with a puzzle.

decline? We spend our lives involved in pursuits of all kinds, both personal and professional. The inclination to be active and involved in things does not change as we age."

Activity aides or assistants may be responsible for preparing equipment and supplies or setting up the activity space. During the activity, they are on hand to assist residents or patients, motivate people to participate, and provide any other help that might be needed. They make sure that patients are safe and that their particular needs are taken into consideration. One patient may need more help or supervision than another. An aide can provide this assistance while the activities director is running the activity with the larger group. The aide may also keep records of equipment and supplies and help plan programs.

Activities directors have bachelor's degrees, but aides or assistants can often start out with just a high school diploma. If they help with certain activities such as swimming, they may need to have special certification and training, such as lifeguard training or CPR training. Over time, they may decide to take classes to help them work with populations such as the elderly or disabled. Working as an aide is a good way to get some knowledge of the field and to get started.

With a general idea of the kinds of jobs available in the human services field, it's helpful to take a step closer and see what a day in the life of human services workers is like.

Chapter Three

A DAY IN THE LIFE

What is it actually like to work in some of the different types of human services jobs? And what particular skills, personality traits, and aptitudes are best for these kinds of jobs? Below we will look at daily life in a number of human services jobs and discuss the skills and qualities needed to succeed in them.

Social Services Administrative Assistant

One entry-level position in human services is that of an administrative assistant to a social worker or group of social workers. An administrative assistant may handle many of the duties of a secretary or reception-ist, as well as additional duties related to the human services aspect of the job. In addition to opening mail, handling incoming phone calls, ordering supplies, and scheduling appointments, the assistant may generate billing for clients and insurance companies, transcribe

A case worker in a family human services agency may assist clients with issues like welfare, unemployment compensation, and other aid programs.

notes and file documents in client charts, and type legal documents needed for court.

Working as an administrative assistant in a social services environment can sometimes be stressful.

Days can be chaotic, and it can be difficult to get everything done with frequent interruptions. While the day may start simply with printing out the social workers' schedules and processing notes, it can be easy to get sidetracked by clients, phone calls, and billing inquiries. However, it can also be rewarding to see clients reach their goals and improve their lives. The position requires patience, good communication skills, and a high level of organization.

Child and Family Support Worker

Other assistant positions in human services, such as a child and family support worker in a public school, entail more hands-on work with clients. Often, this position involves being part of a team and working with other professionals to provide children with the help they need. There may be a need to work with par-

Support workers, such as guidance counselors, often help students who are coping with problems at school or at home.

ents, especially for support workers in areas with high rates of poverty, abuse, or violence. In some cases, support workers may have to provide basic services that parents simply can't.

In an article on the website Optimus Education, Debbie Todd, a child and family support worker in a primary school, describes one typical workday. The following surprise visit from a parent was just one event in a day packed with meetings, phone calls, and home visits:

> 8:45 AM: [A mother] wanted to know if I could recommend a wig specialist for her daughter, as she "was sick to death of her having nits" and wanted to "shave her hair off." Without going into every detail, we had a long chat on other options that were available and not so extreme and that will have less of a serious impact on her nine-year-old daughter's emotional well-being! The mother was adamant that she was going to do this, but agreed to speak to our school nurse if I could arrange it today. Phew!

In their role as counselors for parents and children and as members of a team, support workers must be able to recognize problems and determine the best ways to deal with them. They need to be good communicators and to have patience. They may have to deal with parents who are suspicious about any kind of social services for their children. They may also have to manage unpleasant situations, such as family abuse or drug and alcohol addictions. They need to be strong and professional in dealing with those kinds of interactions.

At the same time, it can also be very rewarding to work with children and families to create the best educational experience possible. Todd says, "I thoroughly enjoy and am extremely passionate about all of my work in school, and I have certainly witnessed how good intervention…improves the lives of children and their families."

LEARNING THE LANGUAGE

One skill that will help students interested in a human services career, particularly in urban areas, is speaking a second language. If there is a large population of people in the community who speak Spanish, Chinese, Korean, or some other language, there will be a need for human services personnel who speak their language. In preparing for a human services career, it will be helpful to take classes in a foreign language that is spoken locally.

Child Care Worker

A child care worker is a human services position that is open to students right out of high school. Child care workers are responsible for the care and supervision of children when they aren't with their families. The position involves taking care of children in a day care center, a preschool, or a school setting, or even in a corporate facility, government agency, hospital, or fitness center. Child care workers also include nannies in private homes and people who take care of children within their own homes.

Some child care workers have set hours in schools or facilities. Others, especially those who work in private homes, may be working around

Teens who like to work with young children often enroll in vo-tech programs in early childhood education. They can then work in day care or other child care settings.

the clock. They may even be employed on a live-in basis. Workers like these are often responsible for some household chores and cooking as well as child care. Most will be with children from early morning through the afternoon. They will supervise meals, games, exercise, and sometimes learning activities, homework, or studying, depending on the age of the child. They may also have to deal with children who are sick or injured, have behavioral issues, or are very active. With young children, "Anything can happen and anything will," says one child care worker on the website of the Princeton Review.

Emily Yoffe of Slate.com temporarily tried the career and wrote a column about her experiences. In the article "Diaper Genie," she describes some of the moments in her day at a day care center:

> During lunchtime with the [youngest children], the women keep an eye on the crawling children and contain the others in a playpen or bouncy seats while they heat up the individual lunches the parents bring. Each woman feeds children in high chairs, two at a time. At mealtime they are like waitresses at some outlandish restaurant where you not only have to spoon the food into the patrons' mouths, but wipe their bottoms afterward. I gave the babies bottles, and one by one they conked out in my arms, and I placed them in their cribs. At 1 PM the women lowered the shades, and all the [babies] were asleep.

To work in child care, most people will need to have good health, good references, and no criminal record. Skills required for the job include patience and maturity but also a love for children and appreciation of what it's like to be a child. They also have to be able to function well with a minimum of adult contact during the day. Also helpful, and sometimes required, are courses in first aid and CPR, as well as early childhood education, child development, and nutrition. Despite some of the challenges, the rewards are great, especially for people who love children. Yoffe writes, "If you work in child care, every hour will provide sweet moments of helping a child."

Halfway House Residential Assistant

Another entry-level human services job is working as an assistant in a halfway house or group home for recovering addicts or ex-convicts. At these residential group homes, people get help dealing with their addictions and returning to everyday life. Recovering addicts are generally given a period of time, usually about six months, to remain drug-free and attend drug and alcohol education to learn how to keep from lapsing. Former prisoners get help finding jobs and readjusting to normal lifestyles. Most halfway houses have a resident director, as well as one or more assistants or aides who may or may not live on-site. These workers assist with the running of the house and the management of the clients.

Because a halfway house or group home houses clients who have had difficulties with drugs, alcohol, or crime, there is usually a strict schedule for the day and firm rules to follow. Those who run the facility want residents to feel at home, but they also want them to do what they need to do in order to recover. A strict schedule is often the best way to give residents the structure they need to succeed.

These residents at a halfway house for substance abusers are meeting in a group run by the residential director.

In most homes, residents get up as early as 5:00 or 6:00 AM. They might have a morning meditation or meeting before leaving to attend school, meetings, work, or counseling. They usually return to the house by 5:00 or 6:00 PM for dinner and time spent together as a group. They must be back in the house for the night by a specific curfew time. The residents also have assigned chores and take turns cooking. Robin Missouri, who is a residential director for a women's halfway house in Baltimore, Maryland, told a reporter from the Morgan State University *Spokesman*, "Because they lived so irresponsibly in the past, this [routine] is a true eye-opener for so many women."

Residential assistants help the resident director with running the house, ordering supplies, keeping records and doing necessary paperwork, and counseling clients. They work to make residents feel at home so that they can acquire a new set of life skills and tools to help them stay clean once they move back into the real world. They may have to deal with residents who break rules or are resistant to treatment. They may need to be on hand for emergency counseling at any time of the day or night.

John, an assistant house manager at a halfway house in Framingham, Massachusetts, describes his job duties on the South Middlesex Opportunity Council's website:

> If one of the men in the house is suspected of using drugs, I give [him] a urine test. So far everyone who's taken the test has been clean. People have responsibilities in the house—cleaning the floors, cleaning the bathroom, things like that. Debbie, the manager, and I both keep an eye on those types of things. If they're starting to slack off, then we talk about it. Every week we have a Monday meeting, when everyone in the house gets together to discuss the week and any issues or problems that need to be brought up.

For human services assistants who work in halfway houses for former prison inmates, there is an added responsibility. They must make sure that the residents follow strict security rules. Some house residents may not have technically been released from their prison sentences yet. Some are not allowed to leave the house at all. Others can leave but must stay within a certain distance from the house and must be in phone contact the entire time.

Aides and assistants in group homes may have to go through more detailed background checks and meet more requirements than workers in other areas. They will most likely have a criminal background check. They may be required to have a driver's license and will need a clean driving record. As with other areas in human services, they need good communication skills, a strong sense of responsibility, and the ability to manage their time well. They also need patience and understanding, as well as a strong desire to help others.

There are many different ways to start a career in human services right out of high school. There are a wide variety of work situations, hours, and job duties. Once a student has decided on a specific human services area, what can he or she do to get started on the path toward that job?

Chapter Four

EXPLORING YOUR VO-TECH OPTIONS

Kaitlyn Chandler is just two years out of high school, but she is already working as a licensed nursing assistant (LNA). She spends time in the homes of elderly and infirm people. She helps them with everyday tasks such as bathing and dressing, laundry, housekeeping, and cooking. She might drive her clients to doctor's appointments. She can choose her hours and how much she wants to work every week, such as working an overnight shift from 7:00 PM to 7:00 AM.

How did Kaitlyn Chandler start working so quickly after graduating from high school? She told Rosen Publishing that she spent her last two years splitting her time between her regular high school and a special regional technical or "career" high school. In her two years there, she took courses in health care, spent time working in a nursing home with residents, and had the opportunity to explore several career paths. She watched several medical operations taking place, shadowed a dental hygienist, and worked with elderly people in an exercise pool at the local wellness center.

Her internship at the nursing home included working with two elderly residents. She bathed, dressed, and fed them for two hours every day. In her senior year of high school, she took advanced classes in health care and was able to become licensed as an LNA before she graduated. Kaitlyn left high school and stepped right into a human services career.

What Is Vo-Tech?

A vo-tech school is shorthand for a vocational-technical high school, which might also be called a career school or a technical center. Many of these schools are now referred to as career and technical education (CTE) schools. These can be special stand-alone schools, like the one Kaitlyn Chandler attended, or programs within regular high schools. The curriculum is focused on teaching students specific working skills that they can use to get jobs without necessarily going on to higher education after high school. For students who aren't interested in college or have a firm career goal in mind, these schools offer more options than a traditional high school.

Since the passage of the Carl D. Perkins Career and Technical Education Act in 2006, states are required by law to make vocational-technical training available to their students. Some high schools are big enough to incorporate technical training into their curriculum. Other districts offer regional vo-tech schools, where students come from surrounding high schools, either part-time or full-time. Schools that send students to a regional vo-tech center have to provide transportation for these students. In some cases, students can spend a half day at a regular high school and a half day at the vo-tech. They can still participate in sports and other extracurricular activities at their home school.

Students who are interested in attending a dedicated, stand-alone vo-tech school often have to submit an application. Since these schools are focused on helping students get jobs and start careers, they want to make sure potential students are well suited for their particular program.

Schools may offer programs of study in any of sixteen different career tracks, which are called career clusters. These career clusters have been recognized by the Office of Vocational and Adult Education (OVAE) and the National Association of State Directors of Career Technical Education Consortium. Examples of career clusters include:

- Agriculture, food, and natural resources
- Architecture and construction
- Arts, A/V technology, and communications
- Business management and administration
- Health science
- Hospitality and tourism
- Human services
- Information technology

Within the sixteen career clusters are seventy-nine career pathways, which are the specialized areas within the fields. Some schools also offer a pre-technical studies program that allows students explore a number of different careers.

Most vo-tech programs include a cooperative piece as well. Cooperative education combines classroom studies with practical work experience. Students practice their skills by interning, volunteering, or working for businesses related to their program of study, such as nursing homes, restaurants, or construction crews.

According to the National Association of State Directors of Career Technical Education Consortium, the career cluster for human services focuses on "preparing individuals for employment in career pathways that relate to families and human needs." The career

As part of her practical work experience for her vo-tech early childhood education class, this student works directly with children in day care.

pathways within human services include: early childhood development and services; counseling and mental health services; family and community services; personal care services; and consumer services.

For students interested in the early childhood career pathway, many vo-tech schools have on-site, accredited day care facilities, where students can work and get a real-world taste of the career. By observing professionals and getting hands-on experience, students learn what it is really like to be a counselor or day care worker. After graduation, students can move directly into jobs as an early childhood education aide or assistant, day care worker, home child care provider, or nanny.

In the Classroom

Choosing a vo-tech program of study isn't a substitute for taking regular academic high school classes. Students usually follow a regular high school curriculum for the first year or two, completing their required classes in subjects such as English, social studies, math, and science. But as they approach their junior year, they can decide on a vo-tech program that they're interested in and focus more on classes in that area.

Students interested in the family and community services pathway, for example, will follow a specific program of study. In the ninth and tenth grades, they take introductory courses in human services and technology applications. In eleventh grade, they take courses in human growth and development, parent and child growth

Vo-tech high school programs, especially for junior and senior level students, require students to take specific classes in their field.

and development, or early childhood education. By senior year, students take special elective courses in family and community services, as well as psychology, economics, or personal finance. They may also take advanced math courses such as statistics or trigonometry. Students graduate from high school with the required academic courses and a good grounding in subjects specific to their career path.

Each career pathway has a clear program of regular high school courses and specialized vo-tech courses that students need to take. A guidance counselor can help students design their specific program of classes to meet both requirements.

In the Field

One of the biggest advantages of attending a vo-tech school is the opportunity for students to work in real-world settings related to their human services interest. Some vo-tech schools actually have on-site work settings such as day care centers, restaurants, and cosmetology salons. Most schools have partnerships with local businesses that are willing to accept vo-tech students, either as paid or unpaid interns, volunteers, or part-time workers. Some of these programs are apprenticeships in which students receive training from professionals in the field. There may also be opportunities for job shadowing. Students have the chance to follow professionals during their daily routines and see firsthand what their jobs are really like. Some students find part-time employment in day care centers, nursing homes, or residential facilities, and then move into full-time jobs at those same facilities

A HIGHER LEVEL OF EDUCATION

In the past, there was often a stigma attached to enrollment in a vocational-technical program. It was sometimes believed that only lower-track students went into these classes. However, today, most vo-tech programs offer challenging courses resulting in marketable career skills and certification in different career areas. The statistics look great for students who enroll in and graduate from vo-tech programs in high school.

- According to the U.S. Department of Education, 90 percent of the students in high school vo-tech programs graduate, compared with only 75 percent of high school students nationwide.

- The National Centers for Career and Technical Education found that vo-tech education students take more and higher-level math than students in general education.

- The Russell Sage Foundation found that vo-tech education graduates are 10 to 15 percent more likely to be in the labor force and earn 8 to 9 percent more than graduates of regular high school programs.

- According to the Georgetown Center on Education and the Workforce, of the forty-seven million job openings expected by 2018, nearly all will require the type of real-world skills that can be learned through a vo-tech program.

after graduation. Not only do students benefit from these hands-on opportunities, but employers can also find new workers.

Each type of internship, apprenticeship, or job shadowing program has specific guidelines. For example,

Students who participate in job shadowing will spend their days working with a professional, learning about their job, asking questions, and discussing aspects of their work.

y Technical Center in Springfield, Vermont,
ollowing types of cooperative agreements
s students and local business partners. Stu-
have job shadowing experiences, which are
-time visits to a company that the student
is interested in. They get to see firsthand
what goes on at the company, and these
visits can sometimes lead to other learning opportunities at that company. Students can also participate in unpaid work
experiences. These are also fairly short in
duration, usually only about thirty hours.
However, unlike job shadowing, students
actually do work within the company, even
though they aren't paid. These work experiences can take place for just a few
hours a week for a number of weeks or in
larger chunks of time. It's the students'
first chance to practice the skills they
learn in the classroom in a real-world
environment.

The next step up from an unpaid career work experience is a paid work experience. Here, the student is actually doing
a job and getting paid for it. These jobs
can last from a few weeks to a semester
to an entire year. Sometimes this kind of
work experience can lead to a permanent
full-time job right after graduation.

There may also be additional requirements for students involved in these
career activities, such as keeping a work

experience journal, getting an evaluation from the employer, or receiving a grade for their participation.

Vo-tech students have an edge over many other students seeking internships and work experiences. A vo-tech school often has established relationships with businesses. Those businesses know that the school's students are actively considering working in the human services field and that they are likely to take their internships or jobs seriously. Also, vo-tech students are typically able to do internships and other work experiences during the school year. Students in traditional high schools and colleges often have to do their internships during the summer, so landing internships during these months is more competitive.

Beyond Vo-Tech

Graduating from a vo-tech school gives students a definite advantage in the workplace. Many students may have taken college-level courses. Many vo-tech schools have partnerships with community colleges or technical schools, and their high school students can attend higher-level courses without having to pay tuition. A vo-tech diploma can also help a student prepare for higher education. Some students might work for a few years at an entry-level job and then decide to go to college for a degree that will let them advance in their field. While it used to be an accepted idea that vo-tech training was only for getting a job, now it is often a head start on a college education. And certification in a field such as child care or preschool education can enable a student to make money at a

For students who have had vo-tech training or earned certificates, there are often jobs waiting for them immediately after high school graduation.

job while either saving for college or attending college part-time.

For students who really aren't interested in going to college or need a job to finance their higher education, a vo-tech school will also have job placement resources and career counseling. Again, this is based on the school's relationships with businesses in the surrounding community or area. According to the vocational-technical schools website for Salem County, New Jersey (http://www.scvts.org), a vo-tech education is valued by most employers because they know those students have the skills needed in the workplace. These skills include:

- Core academic skills and the ability to apply those skills to concrete situations
- Employability skills, such as critical thinking and responsibility, that are essential in any career area
- Job-specific, technical skills related to a specific career pathway

Once students have a vo-tech high school diploma in hand, as well as any related certifications in the field, they are ready to move into their new career. And the possibilities are only just beginning.

Chapter Five

VO-TECH AND BEYOND

The big day comes: high school graduation. Some students are going straight to college in the fall. Others are joining the military. Still others will start working full-time immediately. For students who attend a vo-tech program, chances are good that they will start working right away. They might even have a job already.

Entry-Level Jobs

Graduating high school seniors who have completed a human services curriculum have several choices as far as getting a job. If they are interested in taking care of young children, they can go to work as an assistant in a day care center, a home-based child care worker, or a live-in nanny. Those interested in slightly older kids can work as an educational aide in a classroom or other school facility. For those interested in adult populations, there are opportunities to work in nursing homes, residential facilities for the elderly or handicapped, or halfway houses for substance abusers or

A student who has graduated from a vo-tech program in child care may find work as a nanny in a private home.

released prisoners. The good news is that all of these career options are in areas that have a shortage of workers, especially workers with training and perhaps certification as well.

Once graduates have a job, their employers will likely provide extensive on-the-job training. Candidates who have certification or have completed a vo-tech program won't require as much training as someone with no experience or training at all. But even vo-tech graduates will receive additional training that is tailored to working in a specific environment or with specific clients. Even though they may need additional training once they are hired, vo-tech students with career education may start at a higher salary level or job position than someone with no previous training.

For any human services job, there are specific competencies or skills that are required. According to the National Organization for Human Services, the training and preparation of workers in the human services field includes the following elements:

- Understanding people, their groups, and their interactions
- Understanding the conditions that allow people to succeed or get in the way of healthy living
- Looking at problems and deciding what the best treatments or solutions might be
- Planning, carrying out, and evaluating those treatments
- Paying attention to whether treatments fit with the values and goals of the clients and of the human services mission
- Mastering the process skills for carrying out treatments and services successfully, such as communication, managing interpersonal relationships, managing time, and having self-discipline

Some of these skills can be acquired through one's vo-tech program and on-the-job training. However, advanced skills for higher-level jobs will usually require more education. A vo-tech high school program can be a valuable stepping-stone to this higher education.

Climbing the Ladder

A vo-tech program in high school is likely to help students find a job in their area of interest quickly. However, a vo-tech background will also be useful if students decide, after working in the field for a while, that they want to aspire to a higher-level position.

There are many human services jobs that require a higher level of education, usually an associate's degree or some amount of college-level vocational or technical training. These jobs include becoming a social work or social services assistant, an entry-level case manager, a community outreach worker, or a mental health assistant.

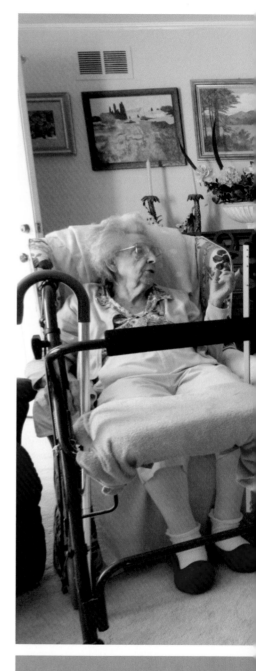

A social worker visits with an elderly woman in her home. Caseworkers are usually required to have advanced college degrees.

A benefit to vo-tech education in high school is that students have often accumulated college credits from their classes. They might be able to attend a community or a four-year college with a number of course credits already under their belt. This makes it faster for these students to acquire a degree. Also, their college education may cost less because they've already taken some of the required courses.

What are some of the typical college degrees that human services workers earn after a vo-tech training background? Which degrees help with job advancement? Associate's degrees generally require only two years past high school to complete. At this level, students can earn an associate of arts (AA), associate of science (AS), or associate of applied science (AAS) degree in human services, depending on the school and the program. These degree programs have different emphases. For example, students earning an AAS degree are more likely to apply their education directly to working with clients. They may study areas such as case management practice and counseling or rehabilitation techniques. They are often hired as paraprofessionals (people who perform part of a professional job but aren't fully licensed as professionals) in social service agencies. They may work in halfway houses, shelters, or group homes.

AA or AS human services degrees are usually more general. They are usually aimed at students who will be working in office environments rather than directly with clients. These degrees emphasize some of the business and administrative aspects of working in human services, such as technology, government regulations, and public policy.

An associate's degree in human services allows students to land a higher-level job than a high school diploma alone. However, these employees will likely still be working under the direct supervision of a social worker, psychologist, or other professional.

A CHANGE IN LANGUAGE

Vo-tech education is increasingly seen not just as a way to help students find work right out of high school but also as a step toward higher education. According to Midcontinent Research for Education and Learning, vocational education used to be seen as a method to train students for low-skilled jobs. Today, it is a way for students to get an education in skilled careers in which they can advance to better and better jobs. This change can be seen in the fact that many schools now call their vo-tech programs "career and technical education," or CTE. They also emphasize that vo-tech education is not just a way to get a job, but a bridge to a career, community college education, or four-year college degree. In many cases, graduating with a vo-tech diploma is just the beginning, not an end in itself.

A Step Higher

For the human services student or worker who wants to continue progressing up the career ladder, the next step is a bachelor's degree. These degrees become even more specialized than an associate's degree. Students can pursue degrees in areas such as psychology, business, sociology, or criminal justice. At this level of education, students need to decide what their career goals are and focus on that specialty.

A professional counselor visits with a client. These counselors usually have a master's or doctorate degree.

For human services workers who want to become professional counselors, social workers, or clinical social workers, even more education is needed, either a master's degree or a doctorate. Again, the areas of study become further specialized. Master's degrees are awarded in concentrations such as marriage and family services, nonprofit management, health and wellness, or executive leadership.

Earning a bachelor's or master's degree might look very far off to someone who is starting as a human services assistant and doesn't have a postsecondary degree. But depending on what the person's career goals are, additional education to earn that college or graduate degree is not only helpful, it is often necessary. Someone working as a residential aide might want to advance to being a residential director. A day care worker might decide that he or she wants to open his or her own day care facility. Both of these jobs require college degrees.

A Last Word

No matter where a student wants to go in the human services field, participating in a vo-tech program is extremely valuable. High school doesn't have to be a period of marking time until graduation comes and one enters the "real" world. For students who know that they're interested in working in human services, a vo-tech program can be a golden opportunity to get a head start on that career. It can make the high school years productive and

As this student works with an elderly woman on her computer skills, he may also be training for a future career in human services.

interesting. A program can be a training ground for a well-paying job or even a head start on a college degree. In a difficult economy, it can be a way to start on a college degree without having to pay college tuition.

The human services field is going to need more and more workers. It is one of the fastest-growing areas of employment, according to the U.S. Department of Labor. From 2010 to 2020, human services assistant jobs alone will grow by 28 percent, faster than the average growth for all occupations. Increasing numbers of human services workers will be needed, and at the moment, there aren't enough workers to fill those jobs. So if a teen thinks that he or she would like to work in this field, it's a great time to get started, and the first step may be right in the student's own high school. Get started on a career with a great future. The time is now!

Glossary

accredited Describes an organization or curriculum that is officially recognized or authorized as maintaining quality standards.

administrative Relating to the running of a business or organization.

agency A business or organization that is established to provide a service.

assess To evaluate or estimate the nature or ability of someone or something.

certification A document attesting that someone has met a certain standard or level for professional conduct and knowledge.

client A person using the services of a human services professional such as a social worker or therapist.

correctional Relating to the treatment and rehabilitation of criminal offenders.

CPR Abbreviation for cardiopulmonary resuscitation, an emergency procedure used to restore normal breathing after cardiac arrest.

dexterity Skill and ease in performing physical tasks, especially with the hands.

diagnose To identify a disease, illness, or condition by signs and symptoms.

hygiene Conditions or practices, such as maintaining cleanliness in personal habits and surroundings, that promote good health.

infirm Someone who is weak or frail because of age or illness.

intervention A measure or treatment carried out to prevent harm or improve functioning.

motivate To provide someone with a reason for doing something.

paraprofessional A person who assists with or performs a particular part of a professional job but is not fully qualified as a professional.

rehabilitation The act of restoring someone to good health or a useful life, usually through therapy or education.

strategy A plan of action or policy designed to achieve a goal.

terminal Incurable; expected to lead to death.

transcribe To put thoughts, speech, or data into a written or printed form.

For More Information

American Public Human Services Association (APHSA)
1133 19th Street NW, Suite 400
Washington, DC 20036
(202) 682-0100
Website: http://www.aphsa.org
APHSA works for excellence in health and human ser-
    vices by supporting state and local agencies, inform-
    ing policymakers, and developing solutions in policy
    and practice. It hosts a job bank for members.

Canadian Association of Social Workers (CASW)
383 Parkdale Avenue, Suite 402
Ottawa, ON K1Y 4R4
Canada
(613) 729-6668
Website: http://www.casw-acts.ca
This organization monitors working conditions and
    establishes standards of practice for social workers
    in Canada. It has a related organization for social
    work students, the Canadian Association for Social
    Work Education (http://www.caswe-acfts.ca).

CARF Canada
10665 Jasper Avenue, Suite 760
Edmonton, AB T5J 3S9
Canada
(780) 429-2538
Website: http://www.carf.org
CARF is an international organization that accredits
    human services providers and provides information
    on them to clients.

National Human Services Assembly
1101 14th Street NW, Suite 600
Washington, DC 20005
(202) 347-2080
Website: http://www.nassembly.org
The National Human Services Assembly is an asso-
    ciation of national nonprofit groups in the fields of
    health, human and community development, and
    human services. Members share knowledge and
    expertise about their work in this sector.

National Organization for Human Services (NOHS)
1600 Sarno Road, Suite 16
Melbourne, FL 32935
Website: http://www.nationalhumanservices.org
This organization for human services professionals
    offers certification, professional development, and
    educational information.

Websites

Due to the changing nature of Internet links, Rosen
Publishing has developed an online list of websites related to the subject of this book. This site is updated
regularly. Please use this link to access the list:

http://www.rosenlinks.com/TRADE/Human

For Further Reading

Barker, Geoff. *Health and Social Care Careers* (In the Workplace). Mankato, MN: Amicus, 2011.

Cohn, Jessica. *Education and Social Services* (Top Careers in Two Years). New York, NY: Ferguson, 2008.

Corey, Marianne Schneider, and Gerald Corey. *Becoming a Helper*. 6th ed. Belmont, CA: Brooks/Cole, Cengage Learning, 2011.

DuBois, Brenda, and Karla Krogsrud Miley. *Social Work: An Empowering Profession*. 8th ed. Boston, MA: Pearson, 2014.

Ferguson Publishing. *Careers in Focus: Social Work*. 3rd ed. New York, NY: Ferguson, 2010.

Flath, Camden. *Social Workers: Finding Solutions for Tomorrow's Society* (New Careers for the 21st Century). Broomall, PA: Mason Crest Publishers, 2011.

Flath, Camden. *21st-Century Counselors: New Approaches to Mental Health & Substance Abuse* (New Careers for the 21st Century). Broomall, PA: Mason Crest Publishers, 2011.

Garner, Geraldine O. *Careers in Social and Rehabilitation Services*. 3rd ed. New York, NY: McGraw-Hill, 2008.

Gillam, Scott. *Human Services* (Field Guides to Finding a New Career). New York, NY: Ferguson Publishing, 2010.

Grabinski, C. Joanne. *101 Careers in Gerontology*. New York, NY: Springer Publishing, 2007.

Grobman, Linda May. *Days in the Lives of Social Workers: 58 Professionals Tell "Real-Life" Stories from Social Work Practice*. 4th ed. Harrisburg, PA: White Hat Communications, 2012.

Kirst-Ashman, Karen Kay. *Introduction to Social Work & Social Welfare: Critical Thinking Perspectives*. Belmont, CA: Brooks/Cole, Cengage Learning, 2013.

LeCroy, Craig Winston. *The Call to Social Work: Life Stories*. 2nd ed. Thousand Oaks, CA: SAGE Publications, 2012.

Martin, Michelle E. *Introduction to Human Services: Through the Eyes of Practice Settings*. 3rd ed. Boston, MA: Pearson Education, 2014.

Morrill, Ann. *Nonprofit Organizations* (Career Launcher). New York, NY: Ferguson, 2011.

Ritter, Jessica A., Halaevalu F. Ofahengaue Vakalahi, and Mary Kiernan-Stern. *101 Careers in Social Work*. New York, NY: Springer Publishing, 2009.

Rosenberg, Jessica. *Working in Social Work: The Real World Guide to Practice Settings*. New York, NY: Routledge, 2009.

Suppes, Mary Ann, and Carolyn Cressy Wells. *The Social Work Experience: An Introduction to Social Work and Social Welfare*. 6th ed. Boston, MA: Pearson, 2013.

Teens' Guide to College & Career Planning: Your High School Roadmap for College & Career Success. 11th ed. Lawrenceville, NJ: Peterson's, 2011.

Zichy, Shoya, and Ann Bidou. *Career Match: Connecting Who You Are with What You'll Love to Do*. New York, NY: AMACOM, 2007.

Bibliography

Belmont, Judy. "Counselor's Role as Teacher and Life Skills Educator." August 1, 2013. Retrieved September 8, 2013 (http://www.belmontwellness. com/counselors-role-teacher-life-skills-educator).

Bureau of Labor Statistics, U.S. Department of Labor. "Social and Human Service Assistants." *Occupational Outlook Handbook*. Retrieved June 16, 2013 (http://www.bls.gov/ooh/community -and-social-service/social-and-human-service -assistants.htm).

Bureau of Labor Statistics, U.S. Department of Labor. "Social Workers." *Occupational Outlook Handbook*. Retrieved September 8, 2013 (http://www.bls.gov/ooh/ community-and-social-service/social-workers.htm).

Chandler, Kaitlyn. Interview with the author. September 11, 2013.

Dunlap, David W. "Halfway House Unobtrusively Preparing Prisoners for Society." *New York Times*, August 11, 1981. Retrieved September 11, 2013 (http://www.nytimes.com/1981/08/11/nyregion/ halfway-house-unobtrusively-preparing-prisoners-for -society.html).

Education Portal. "Life Skills Instructor: Employment Options and Requirements." Retrieved September 8, 2013 (http://education-portal.com/articles/ Life_Skills_Instructor_Employment_Options_and _Requirements.html).

Healthcare Jobs. "Social and Human Service Assistant Jobs and Careers." Retrieved September 11, 2013 (http://www.healthcarejobs.org/social_assistant.htm).

Jacobson, Louis, and Christine Mokher. "Pathways to Boosting the Earnings of Low-Income Students by

Increasing Their Educational Attainment." Hudson Institute Center for Employment Policy, January 2009. Retrieved October 6, 2013 (http://www. hudson.org/files/publications/Pathways%20to%20 Boosting.pdf).

Jones, Allison. "3 Tips for Launching a Career as a Community Organizer." *Idealist Careers*, March 29, 2013. Retrieved September 8, 2013 (http://idealistcareers.org/3-tips-for-launching-a-career-as-a-community-organizer).

Maryland State Department of Education. "Career and Technology Education: Frequently Asked Questions." October 2007. Retrieved September 13, 2013 (http://www.calvertnet.k12.md.us/departments/instruction/cte/documents/ctehighres.pdf).

McMullen, Laura. "Students Excel at Vocational, Technical High Schools." *U.S. News and World Report*, November 11, 2011. Retrieved September 8, 2013 (http://news.yahoo.com/students-excel-vocational-technical-high-schools-161255325.html).

McREL International. "Career Pathways Initiatives." May 10, 2012. Retrieved September 8, 2013 (http://www.mcrel.org/about-us/hot-topics/ht-career-pathways).

Mizrahi, Terry. "Community Organizers: For a Change." Silberman School of Social Work at Hunter College. Retrieved September 8, 2013 (http://www.hunter. cuny.edu/socwork/ecco/cocareer.htm).

Moffat, Colleen Teixeira. "Helping Those in Need: Human Service Workers." *Occupational Outlook Quarterly*, Fall 2011. Retrieved August 17, 2013 (http:// www.bls.gov/opub/ooq/2011/fall/art03.pdf).

MSU Spokesman. "A Half-Way House in the 'Morgan Mile' Helps Recovering Addicts." December 12, 2012. Retrieved September 11, 2013 (http://www.themsuspokesman.com/2012/12/12/a-half-way-house-in-the-morgan-mile-helps-recovering-addicts).

MyFootpath.com. "Human Services Careers." 2011. Retrieved September 7, 2013 (http://myfootpath.com/careers/human-services-careers).

National Association of Social Workers, Ohio Chapter. "A Day in the Life of a Social Worker." Retrieved September 8, 2013 (http://www.naswoh.org/displaycommon.cfm?an=1&subarticlenbr=647).

National Association of State Directors of Career Technical Education Consortium. "Career Clusters & Pathways." Retrieved October 6, 2013 (http://www.careertech.org/career-clusters/glance/clusters-occupations.html).

National Organization for Human Services. "What Is Human Services?" Retrieved June 16, 2013 (http://www.nationalhumanservices.org/what-is-human-services).

O'Neill, Liz. "FAQs for Students Seeking Human Services or Social Work Degrees." eLearners.com, April 2, 2012. Retrieved September 14, 2013 (http://www.elearners.com/online-education-resources/careers/faqs-for-students-seeking-human-services-or-social-work-degrees).

O*Net OnLine. "Summary Report for: 21-1093.00 – Social and Human Service Assistants." 2010. Retrieved June 16, 2013 (http://www.onetonline.org/link/summary/21-1093.00).

Optimus Education. "A Day in the Life of a Child and Family Support Worker in School." October 28, 2009. Retrieved September 11, 2013 (http://www.optimus -education.com/day-life-child-and-family-support -worker-school).

Paggi, Kay. "Activity Directors' Tips for Creating Meaningful Senior Activities." Caring.com. Retrieved September 9, 2013 (http://www.caring.com/articles/ senior-activity-guide-activity-directors-tips-elderly -activities).

Palermo, Sarah. "State Videos Show What Working in Health and Human Services Is Really Like, Aiming to Reduce Turnover." *Concord Monitor*, July 7, 2013. Retrieved September 1, 2013 (http://www .concordmonitor.com/home/7281325-95/state -videos-show-what-working-in-health-and-human -services-is-really-like-aiming).

Princeton Review. "Child Care Worker." Retrieved September 11, 2013 (http://www.princetonreview .com/careers.aspx?cid=35).

Princeton Review. "Social Worker." Retrieved September 7, 2013 (http://www.princetonreview.com/ca- reers.aspx?cid=143).

Rappoport, Ann L. "Not Your Daddy's Vo-Tech." *MetroKids*, May 2011. Retrieved September 8, 2013 (http://www.metrokids.com/MetroKids/May -2011/Not-Your-Daddy-039s-Vo-Tech).

Rimer, Sara. "Community Organizing Never Looked So Good." *New York Times*, April 12, 2009. Retrieved September 8, 2013 (http://www.nytimes. com/2009/04/12/fashion/12organizer.html ?pagewanted=all&_r=0).

River Valley Technical Center. "Human Services." Retrieved September 8, 2013 (http://www.rvtc.org/index.php/programs/human-services).

Salem County Vocational Technical Schools. "What Is Career and Technical Education?" Retrieved September 13, 2013 (http://www.scvts.org/?p=1076).

SMOC Sober Housing, Federal Home Loan Bank of Boston. "The Residents." Retrieved September 8, 2013 (http://www.fhlbboston.com/communitydevelopment/profiles/smoc/residents.jsp).

Stover, Del. "The New Vo-Tech." *American School Board Journal*, August 2013. Retrieved September 10, 2013 (http://www.asbj.com/MainMenuCategory/Archive/2013/August/The-New-Vo-Tech.html).

Yoffe, Emily. "Diaper Genie." Slate.com, June 25, 2008. Retrieved September 7, 2013 (http://www.slate.com/articles/life/human_guinea_pig/2008/06/diaper_genie.html).

Index

A

abuse, 10, 12, 20, 32, 33, 55
accreditation, 46
addiction, 8, 10, 12, 33, 37, 40, 55
AmeriCorps VISTA, 24
apprenticeships, 48, 50
associate's degrees, 6, 9, 17, 58, 60, 61, 62

B

bachelor's degrees, 6, 17, 21, 28, 61, 62, 63
background checks, 41
Belmont, Judy, 22
Bureau of Labor Statistics, 6, 14

C

career and technical education (CTE), 43, 61
career counseling, 53
Carl D. Perkins Career and Technical Education Act, 7, 43
caseworkers, 10, 18, 19–20
certification, 9, 22, 28, 49, 52, 54, 56
Chandler, Kaitlyn, 42–43

child and family support workers, 31–33
child care workers, 34–37, 46, 55
clinical social workers, 19, 20–21, 63
community colleges, 9, 52, 61
community organizers, 23–25
counselors, 9, 10, 33, 46, 48, 60, 63
CPR training, 28, 36
criminal records, 36

D

day care workers, 46, 55, 63
depression, 20, 26
direct-service social workers, 19, 20, 21
disabled people, 4, 6, 8, 12, 15, 20, 22, 28, 55
doctoral degrees, 63
driver's licenses, 22, 41

E

elderly people, 4, 6, 12, 15, 18, 20, 22, 28, 42, 43, 55
entry-level jobs, 9, 17, 29, 37, 52, 55–58

F

family services assistants, 10
first aid, 36
food stamps, 8, 11, 20
four-year degrees, 6, 17, 21, 28, 61

G

Georgetown Center on Education and the Workforce, 49
group activities aides, 26–28
group homes, 14, 26 37–41, 60
group therapy, 21
guidance counselors, 10, 48

H

halfway house residential assistants, 37–41, 55, 60
high school diplomas, 6, 9, 21, 28, 54
homeless people, 4, 15, 24
human services careers
  daily life in, 29–41
  entry-level jobs, 9, 17, 29, 37, 52, 55–58
  as a good fit, 18–28
  overview, 4–17
  succeeding in, 58–65
  vo-tech options, 42–54

I

immigrants, 4, 6, 14
internships, 43, 45, 48, 50, 52

J

job shadowing, 48, 50, 51

L

licensed nursing assistants (LNAs), 42, 43
lifeguard training, 28
life skills instructors, 21–23

M

master's degrees, 21, 62, 63
mental illness, 4, 14, 15, 19, 20
Midcontinent Research for Education and Learning, 61
military families, 12–13
Missouri, Robin, 39

N

nannies, 34, 46, 55
National Centers for Career and Technical Education, 49
National Organization for Human Services, 57

nursing homes, 4, 14, 18, 26, 42, 43, 45, 48, 55

O

Obama, Barack, 25
on-the-job training, 56–57

P

Paggi, Kay, 26
paraprofessionals, 60
part-time jobs, 4, 15, 48
Peace Corps, 24
Pierre, Anthonine, 24
prisoners, former, 4, 14–15, 22, 37, 40–41, 56
psychologists, 9, 10, 61

R

rehabilitation, 8, 14, 18, 60
residential facilities, 12, 14, 26, 37–41, 48, 55, 63
River Valley Technical Center, 51
Russell Sage Foundation, 49

S

second language, learning a, 34
shelters, 4, 15, 24, 60
social services administrative assistants, 29–31

social workers, 9, 10, 18–21, 29, 31, 61, 63
sociologists, 9, 10
special needs children, 22
substance abuse counselors, 10
support groups, 12, 14

T

technical certificates, 9
Todd, Debbie, 32–33
two-year degrees, 6, 17, 58, 60, 61, 62

U

U.S. Department of Education, 49
U.S. Department of Labor, 65

V

veterans, 12, 13, 15
volunteering, 4, 24, 45, 48

W

welfare, 11

Y

Yoffe, Emily 36, 37

About the Author

Marcia Amidon Lusted is the author of eighty-five books and over four hundred magazine articles for young readers. She is an assistant editor for Cobblestone Publishing, a writing instructor, and a musician. She lives in New Hampshire.

Photo Credits

Cover (figure) © iStockphoto.com/DRB Images, LLC; cover (background), pp. 1, 3 Joe Raedle/Getty Images; p. 5 Education Images/Universal Images Group/Getty Images; p. 9 Craig F. Walker/The Denver Post/Getty Images; p. 11 Helen H. Richardson/The Denver Post/Getty Images; pp. 12–13 The Christian Science Monitor/Getty Images; pp. 16–17, 19, 30–31 © AP Images; p. 23 Robyn Beck/AFP/Getty Images; p. 25 Obama for America/AP Images; pp. 26–27 David Ramos/Getty Images; p. 32 © Burger/Phanie/The Image Works; p. 35 Thomas Lohnes/Getty Images; pp. 38–39 © Robin Nelson/PhotoEdit; p. 45 © Billy E. Barnes/PhotoEdit; p. 47 Goodluz/Shutterstock .com; pp. 50–51 Photofusion/Universal Images Group/Getty Images; p. 53 Armadillo Stock/Shutterstock.com; p. 56 Patrick Heagney/E+/Getty Images; pp. 58–59 The Washington Post/ Getty Images; p. 62 Rob Mamion/Shutterstock.com; pp. 64–65 Bethany Clarke/Getty Images; cover and interior elements Goodluz/Shutterstock.com (child writing), Jirsak/Shutterstock .com (tablet frame), schab/Shutterstock.com (text highlighting), nikifiva/Shutterstock.com (stripe textures), Zfoto/Shutterstock .com (abstract curves); back cover graphics ramcreations/ Shutterstock.com, Artco/Shutterstock (handshake icon).

Designer: Michael Moy; Editor: Andrea Sclarow Paskoff; Photo Researcher: Marty Levick